50 GREATEST HYMNS

- A Mighty Fortress Is Our God
- Abide with Me
- All Creatures of Our God and King
- All Hail the Power of Jesus' Name
- Alleluia! Alleluia! (Ode to Joy)
- Amazing Grace
- Are You Washed in the Blood?
- At the Cross
- Be Thou My Vision
- Blessed Assurance
- Christ Arose (Low in the Grave He Lay)
- Christ the Lord is Risen Today
- Come, Christians, Join to Sing
- Come, Thou Fount of Every Blessing
- Come, Thou Long-Expected Jesus
- Crown Him with Many Crowns
- Down at the Cross
- Fairest Lord Jesus
- He Leadeth Me
- He Lives (I Know That My Redeemer Lives!)
- Holy, Holy, Holy
- How Great Thou Art
- I Stand Amazed in the Presence (How Marvelous)
- In the Garden
- It Is Well with My Soul

- Jesus Loves Me
- Jesus Paid It All
- Jesus Saves
- Just as I Am
- Love Divine, All Loves Excelling
- My Hope Is Built On Nothing Less
- Near the Cross
- Nearer, My God, to Thee
- Nothing but the Blood
- O For A Thousand Tongues To Sing
- O Sacred Head, Now Wounded
- O the Blood of Jesus
- O Worship the King
- Onward, Christian Soldiers
- Rock Of Ages
- Shall We Gather at the River
- Tell Me the Story of Jesus
- The Old Rugged Cross
- There is a Fountain
- To God Be the Glory
- We Gather Together
- Were You There
- What A Friend We Have in Jesus
- What Wondrous Love Is This
- When I Survey the Wondrous Cross

Arranged by B. C. Dockery

A Mighty Fortress Is Our God

Martin Luther
B. C. Dockery

A Mighty Fortress Is Our God

Martin Luther

B. C. Dockery

Flute 1

Arr. ©2022

A Mighty Fortress Is Our God

Flute 2

Martin Luther
B. C. Dockery

A Mighty Fortress Is Our God

Piano

Martin Luther

B. C. Dockery

Score

Abide with Me

William H. Monk
arr. B. C. Dockery

Flute 1

Abide with Me

William H. Monk
arr. B. C. Dockery

Flute 2

Abide with Me

William H. Monk

arr. B. C. Dockery

Abide with Me

William H. Monk
arr. B. C. Dockery

All Creatures of Our God and King

Geistliche Kirchengesang, 1623

arr. B . C. Dockery

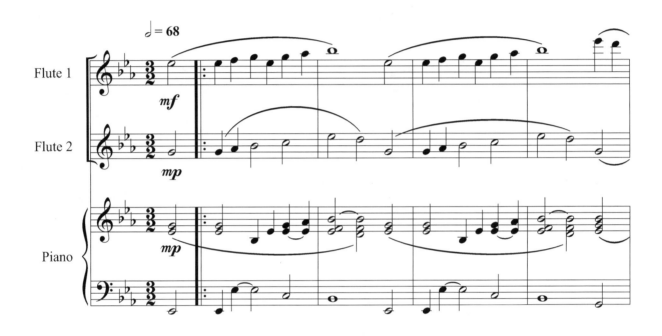

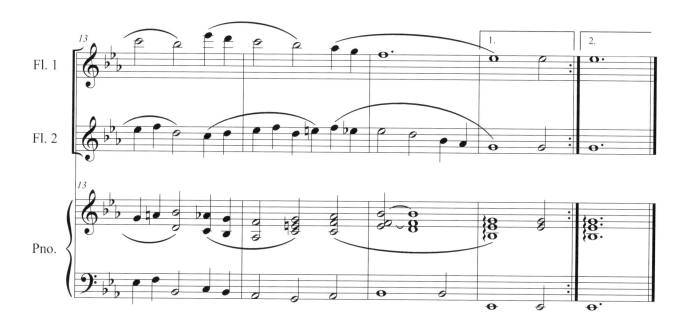

Flute 1

All Creatures of Our God and King

Geistliche Kirchengesang, 1623
arr. B . C. Dockery

Flute 2

All Creatures of Our God and King

Geistliche Kirchengesang, 1623
arr. B . C. Dockery

All Creatures of Our God and King

Geistliche Kirchengesang, 1623

arr. B . C. Dockery

All Hail the Power of Jesus' Name

Oliver Holden

B. C. Dockery

All Hail the Power of Jesus' Name

Oliver Holden

B. C. Dockery

Flute 1

All Hail the Power of Jesus' Name

Oliver Holden

B. C. Dockery

Flute 2

All Hail the Power of Jesus' Name

Piano

Oliver Holden
B. C. Dockery

Arr. ©2022

Ode to Joy
(Joyful, Joyful, We Adore Thee)

Beethoven
arr. B. C. Dockery

Ode to Joy
(Joyful, Joyful, We Adore Thee)

Ode to Joy
(Joyful, Joyful, We Adore Thee)

Flute 1

Beethoven
arr. B. C. Dockery

Ode to Joy
(Joyful, Joyful, We Adore Thee)

Flute 2

Beethoven
arr. B. C. Dockery

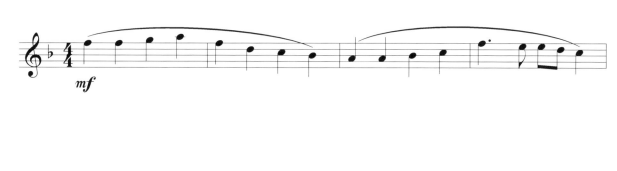

Ode to Joy
(Joyful, Joyful, We Adore Thee)

Beethoven
arr. B. C. Dockery

Amazing Grace

John Newton

B. C. Dockery

Amazing Grace

Flute 1

John Newton
B. C. Dockery

Amazing Grace

Flute 2

John Newton
B. C. Dockery

Amazing Grace

John Newton

B. C. Dockery

Are You Washed in the Blood?

Elisha A. Hoffman
arr. B. C. Dockery

Are You Washed in the Blood?

Elisha A. Hoffman
arr. B. C. Dockery

Flute 1

Are You Washed in the Blood?

Elisha A. Hoffman
arr. B. C. Dockery

Flute 2

Are You Washed in the Blood?

Elisha A. Hoffman
arr. B. C. Dockery

At the Cross

Anon
arr. B. C. Dockery

At the Cross

At the Cross

Flute 1

Anon
arr. B. C. Dockery

At the Cross

Flute 2

Anon
arr. B. C. Dockery

At the Cross

Anon
arr. B. C. Dockery

Be Thou My Vision

Traditional
B. C. Dockery

Arr. ©2022

Be Thou My Vision

Traditional
B. C. Dockery

Flute 1

Be Thou My Vision

Traditional
B. C. Dockery

Flute 2

Arr. ©2022

Be Thou My Vision

Traditional
B. C. Dockery

Piano

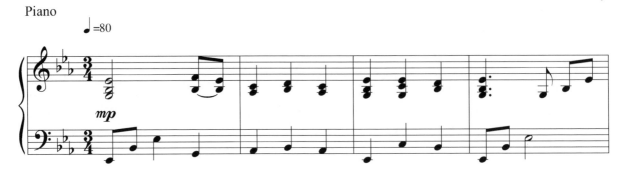

Arr. ©2022

Blessed Assurance

Phoebe P. Knapp
B. C. Dockery

Blessed Assurance

Phoebe P. Knapp

B. C. Dockery

Flute 1

Blessed Assurance

Phoebe P. Knapp

B. C. Dockery

Flute 2

Blessed Assurance

Phoebe P. Knapp

B. C. Dockery

Arr. ©2022

Christ Arose
(Low in the Grave He Lay)

Robert Lowry
arr. B. C. Dockery

Christ Arose
(Low in the Grave He Lay)

Christ Arose
(Low in the Grave He Lay)

Flute 1

Robert Lowry
arr. B. C. Dockery

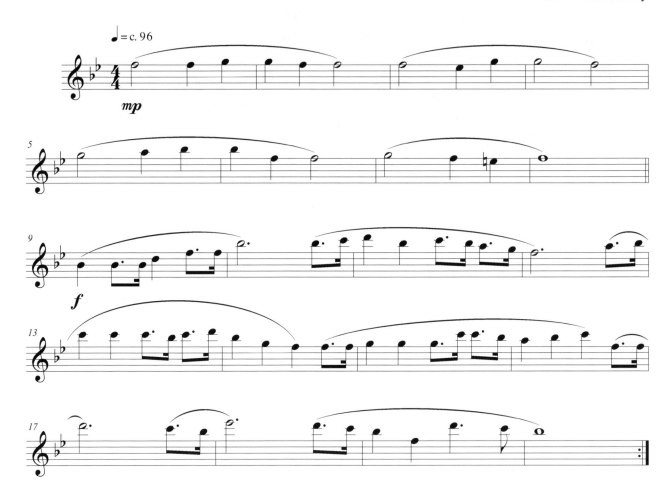

Christ Arose
(Low in the Grave He Lay)

Flute 2

Robert Lowry
arr. B. C. Dockery

Christ Arose
(Low in the Grave He Lay)

Robert Lowry
arr. B. C. Dockery

Piano

Christ the Lord is Risen Today

Charles Wesley
arr. B. C. Dockery

Christ the Lord is Risen Today

Christ the Lord is Risen Today

Flute 1

Charles Wesley
arr. B. C. Dockery

Christ the Lord is Risen Today

Flute 2

Charles Wesley
arr. B. C. Dockery

Christ the Lord is Risen Today

Charles Wesley
arr. B. C. Dockery

Score

Come, Christians, Join to Sing

Traditional Spanish Melody

arr. B. C. Dockery

Flute 1

Come, Christians, Join to Sing

Traditional Spanish Melody
arr. B. C. Dockery

Flute 2

Come, Christians, Join to Sing

Traditional Spanish Melody
arr. B. C. Dockery

Come, Christians, Join to Sing

Traditional Spanish Melody

arr. B. C. Dockery

Come, Thou Fount of Every Blessing

Traditional
B. C. Dockery

Arr. ©2022

Come, Thou Fount of Every Blessing

Traditional
B. C. Dockery

Flute 1

Come, Thou Fount of Every Blessing

Traditional
B. C. Dockery

Flute 2

Arr. ©2022

Come, Thou Fount of Every Blessing

Traditional
B. C. Dockery

Piano

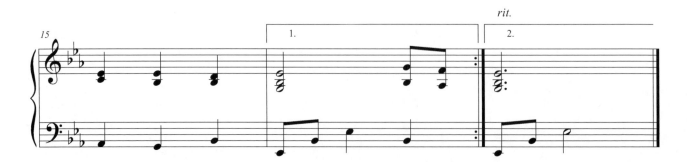

Come, Thou Long-Expected Jesus

Score

Rowland H. Prichard

B. C. Dockery

2

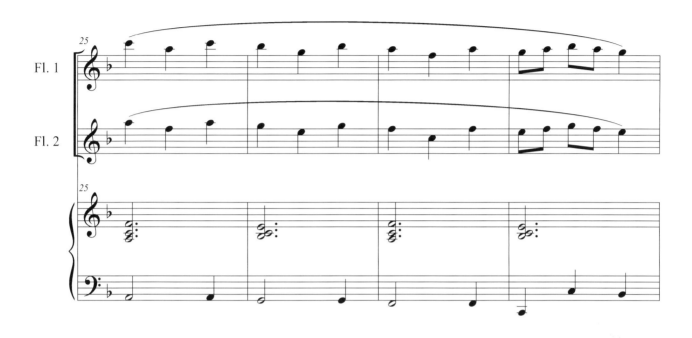

Come, Thou Long-Expected Jesus

Flute 1

Rowland H. Prichard
B. C. Dockery

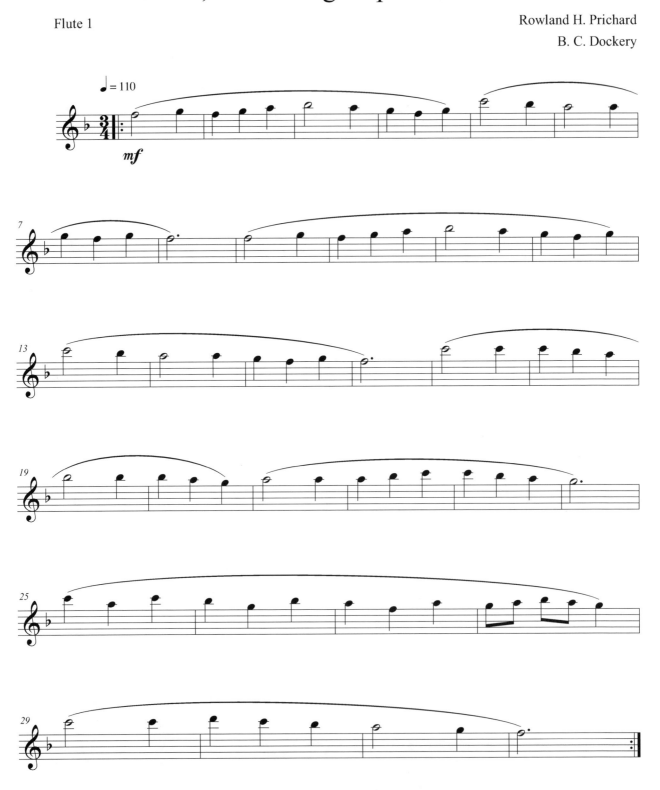

Arr. ©2022

Come, Thou Long-Expected Jesus

Flute 2

Rowland H. Prichard
B. C. Dockery

Come, Thou Long-Expected Jesus

Piano

Rowland H. Prichard
B. C. Dockery

♩ = 110

Crown Him with Many Crowns

George J. Elvey
arr. B. C. Dockery

Crown Him with Many Crowns

Flute 1

George J. Elvey
arr. B. C. Dockery

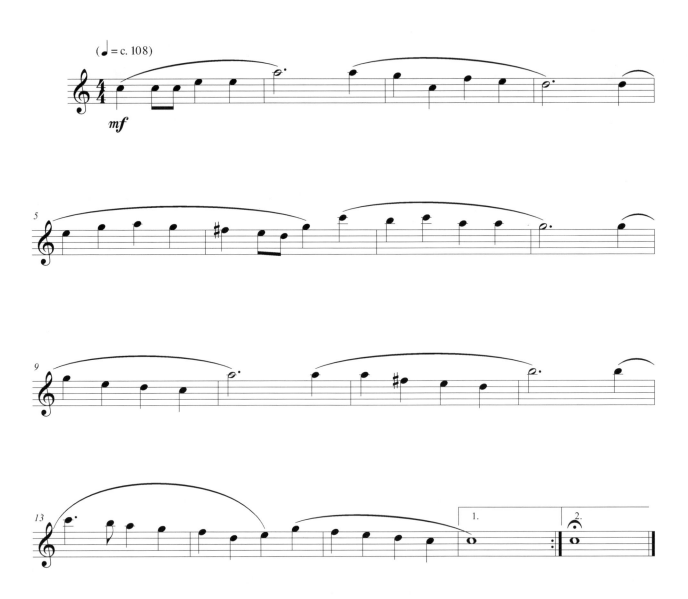

Crown Him with Many Crowns

Flute 2

George J. Elvey
arr. B. C. Dockery

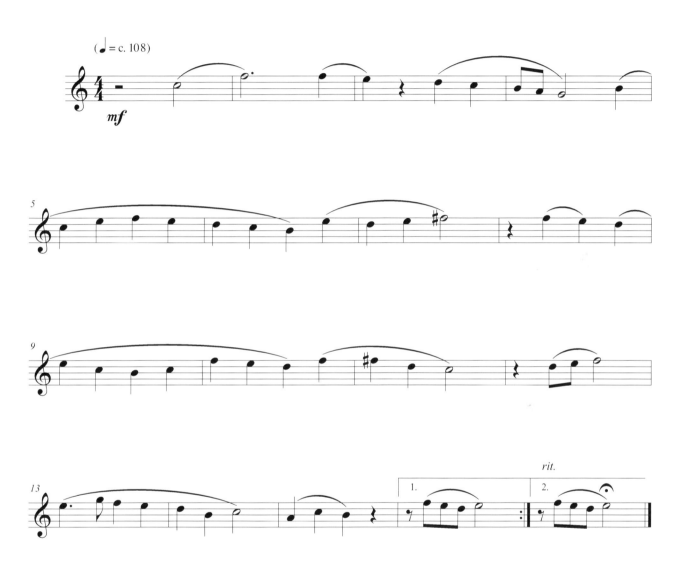

Crown Him with Many Crowns

George J. Elvey
arr. B. C. Dockery

Down at the Cross

John H. Stockton
arr. B. C. Dockery

Down at the Cross

Flute 1

John H. Stockton
arr. B. C. Dockery

Down at the Cross

Flute 2

John H. Stockton
arr. B. C. Dockery

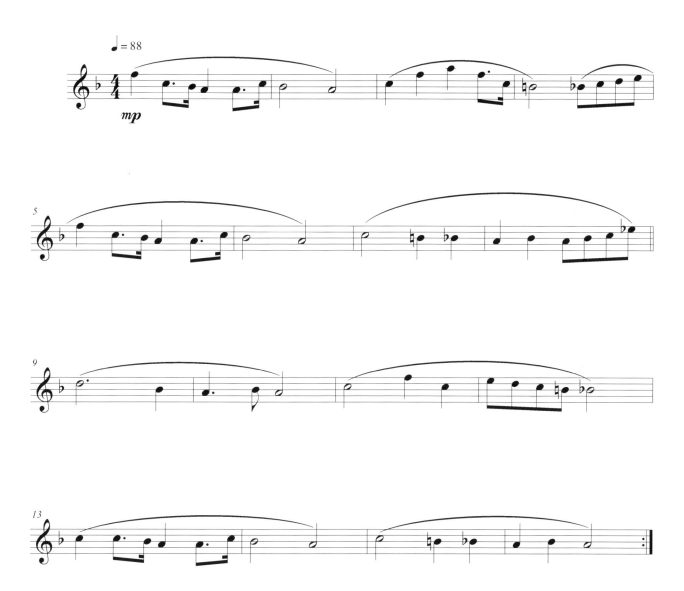

Down at the Cross

John H. Stockton
arr. B. C. Dockery

Score

Fairest Lord Jesus

Silesian Folk Melody
arr. B. C. Dockery

Fairest Lord Jesus

Silesian Folk Melody
arr. B. C. Dockery

Fairest Lord Jesus

Silesian Folk Melody
arr. B. C. Dockery

Fairest Lord Jesus

Silesian Folk Melody
arr. B. C. Dockery

He Leadeth Me

William B. Bradbury

B. C. Dockery

Arr. ©2022

He Leadeth Me

William B. Bradbury
B. C. Dockery

Flute 1

Arr. ©2022

He Leadeth Me

William B. Bradbury
B. C. Dockery

Flute 2

He Leadeth Me

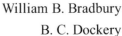

He Lives
(I Know That My Redeemer Lives!)

Samuel Medley
arr. B. C. Dockery

He Lives
(I Know That My Redeemer Lives!)

He Lives
(I Know That My Redeemer Lives!)

Flute 1

Samuel Medley
arr. B. C. Dockery

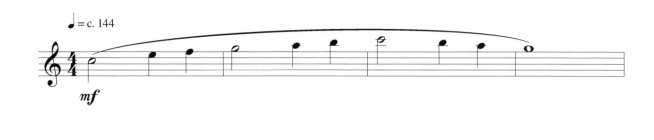

He Lives
(I Know That My Redeemer Lives!)

Flute 2

Samuel Medley
arr. B. C. Dockery

He Lives
(I Know That My Redeemer Lives!)

Samuel Medley
arr. B. C. Dockery

Holy, Holy, Holy

John B. Dykes

Holy, Holy, Holy

Flute 1

John B. Dykes

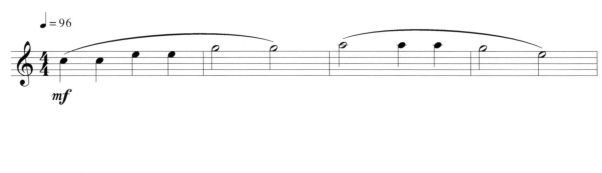

Holy, Holy, Holy

Flute 2

John B. Dykes

Holy, Holy, Holy

John B. Dykes

Score

How Great Thou Art

Traditional
B. C. Dockery

How Great Thou Art

Traditional
B. C. Dockery

Flute 1

Arr. ©2022

How Great Thou Art

Flute 2

Traditional
B. C. Dockery

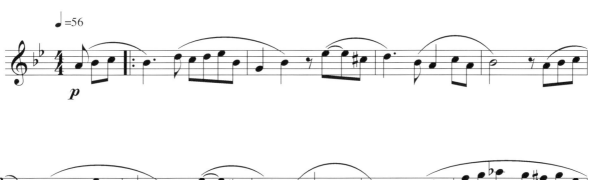

How Great Thou Art

Traditional
B. C. Dockery

Piano

I Stand Amazed in the Presence
(How Marvelous)

Charles H. Gabriel
arr. B. C. Dockery

I Stand Amazed in the Presence
(How Marvelous)

I Stand Amazed in the Presence
(How Marvelous)

Flute 1

Charles H. Gabriel
arr. B. C. Dockery

I Stand Amazed in the Presence
(How Marvelous)

Flute 2

Charles H. Gabriel
arr. B. C. Dockery

I Stand Amazed in the Presence
(How Marvelous)

Charles H. Gabriel
arr. B. C. Dockery

Score

In the Garden

C. Austin Miles

arr. B. C. Dockery

Flute 1

In the Garden

C. Austin Miles

arr. B. C. Dockery

Flute 2

In the Garden

C. Austin Miles
arr. B. C. Dockery

In the Garden

C. Austin Miles
arr. B. C. Dockery

Score

It Is Well with My Soul

Philip P. Bliss

B. C. Dockery

Flute 1

It Is Well with My Soul

Philip P. Bliss
B. C. Dockery

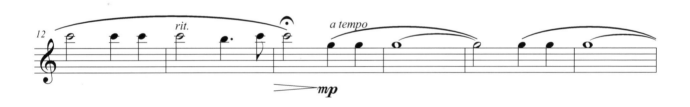

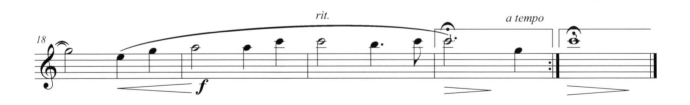

Flute 2

It Is Well with My Soul

Philip P. Bliss
B. C. Dockery

It Is Well with My Soul

Philip P. Bliss
B. C. Dockery

Jesus Loves Me

William B. Bradbury
Arr. B. C. Dockery

Jesus Loves Me

Jesus Loves Me

Flute 1

William B. Bradbury

Jesus Loves Me

Flute 2

William B. Bradbury

Jesus Loves Me

William B. Bradbury

Jesus Paid It All

John T. Grape
arr. B. C. Dockery

Jesus Paid It All

Flute 1

John T. Grape
arr. B. C. Dockery

Jesus Paid It All

Flute 2

John T. Grape
arr. B. C. Dockery

Jesus Paid It All

John T. Grape
arr. B. C. Dockery

Jesus Saves

We Have Heard the Joyful Sound

William J. Kirkpatrick
arr. B. C. Dockery

Jesus Saves
We Have Heard the Joyful Sound

Flute 1

William J. Kirkpatrick
arr. B. C. Dockery

Jesus Saves
We Have Heard the Joyful Sound

Flute 2

William J. Kirkpatrick
arr. B. C. Dockery

Jesus Saves

We Have Heard the Joyful Sound

William J. Kirkpatrick
arr. B. C. Dockery

Score

Just as I Am

William B. Bradbury
B. C. Dockery

Just as I Am

Flute 1

William B. Bradbury
B. C. Dockery

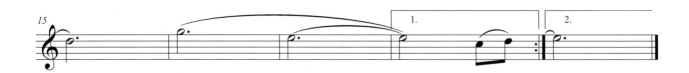

Arr. ©2022

Just as I Am

Flute 2

William B. Bradbury
B. C. Dockery

Arr. ©2022

Just as I Am

Piano

William B. Bradbury
B. C. Dockery

Arr. ©2022

Love Divine, All Loves Excelling

Score

John Zundel

B. C. Dockery

Arr. ©2022

Love Divine, All Loves Excelling

Flute 1

John Zundel

B. C. Dockery

Love Divine, All Loves Excelling

Flute 2

John Zundel
B. C. Dockery

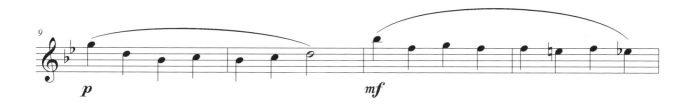

Love Divine, All Loves Excelling

Piano

John Zundel

B. C. Dockery

Arr. ©2022

My Hope Is Built On Nothing Less

Score

William B. Bradbury

B. C. Dockery

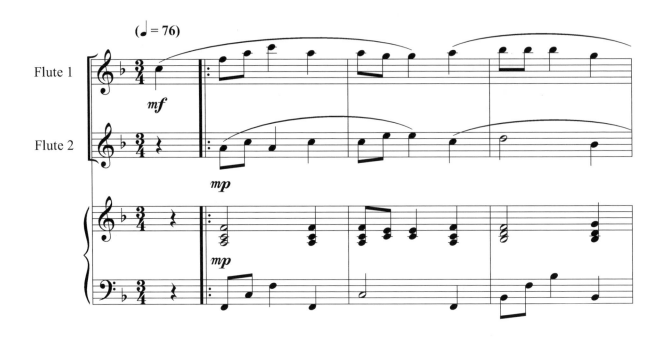

My Hope Is Built On Nothing Less

Flute 1

William B. Bradbury

B. C. Dockery

My Hope Is Built On Nothing Less

Flute 2

William B. Bradbury

B. C. Dockery

My Hope Is Built On Nothing Less

Piano

William B. Bradbury
B. C. Dockery

Near the Cross

William H. Doane
arr. B. C. Dockery

Near the Cross

Flute 1

William H. Doane
arr. B. C. Dockery

Flute 2

Near the Cross

William H. Doane
arr. B. C. Dockery

Near the Cross

William H. Doane
arr. B. C. Dockery

Score

Nearer, My God, to Thee

Lowell Mason

B. C. Dockery

Flute 1

Nearer, My God, to Thee

Lowell Mason

B. C. Dockery

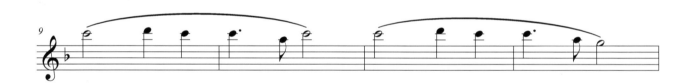

Flute 2

Nearer, My God, to Thee

Lowell Mason
B. C. Dockery

Nearer, My God, to Thee

Lowell Mason

B. C. Dockery

Nothing but the Blood

Robert Lowry
arr. B. C. Dockery

Nothing but the Blood

Flute 1

Robert Lowry
arr. B. C. Dockery

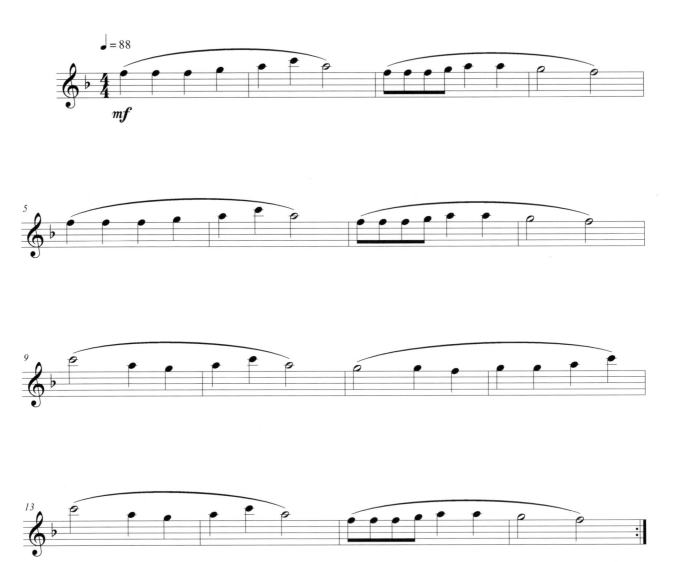

Nothing but the Blood

Flute 2

Robert Lowry
arr. B. C. Dockery

Nothing but the Blood

Robert Lowry
arr. B. C. Dockery

O for a Thousand Toungues to Sing

Score

Carl G. Glazer

B. C. Dockery

Arr. ©2022

O for a Thousand Toungues to Sing

Flute 1

Carl G. Glazer

B. C. Dockery

O for a Thousand Toungues to Sing

Flute 2

Carl G. Glazer
B. C. Dockery

O for a Thousand Toungues to Sing

Piano

Carl G. Glazer

B. C. Dockery

O Sacred Head, Now Wounded

Hans Leo Hassler; harmonized by J. S. Bach
arr. B. C. Dockery

O Sacred Head, Now Wounded

Flute 1

Hans Leo Hassler; harmonized by J. S. Bach

arr. B. C. Dockery

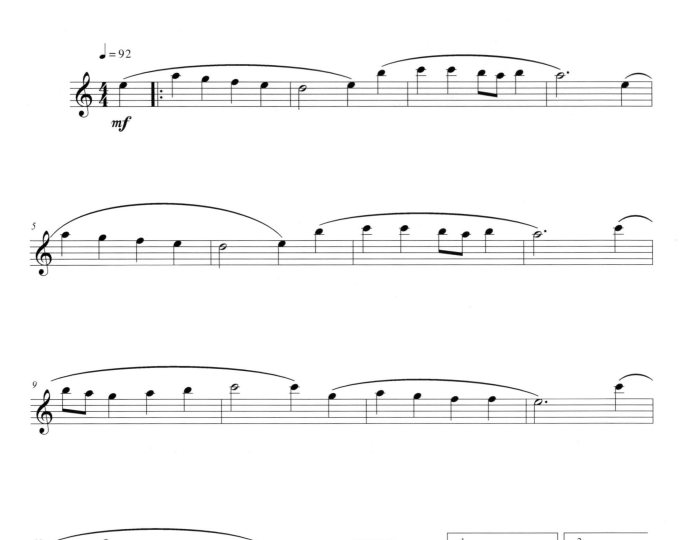

O Sacred Head, Now Wounded

Flute 2

Hans Leo Hassler; harmonized by J. S. Bach

arr. B. C. Dockery

O Sacred Head, Now Wounded

Hans Leo Hassler; harmonized by J. S. Bach

arr. B. C. Dockery

O the Blood

Traditional
arr. B. C. Dockery

O the Blood

Flute 1

Traditional
arr. B. C. Dockery

O the Blood

Flute 2

Traditional
arr. B. C. Dockery

O the Blood

Piano

Traditional
arr. B. C. Dockery

Score

O Worship the King

Attr. Kraus & Haydn
B. C. Dockery

Flute 1

O Worship the King

Attr. Kraus & Haydn
B. C. Dockery

O Worship the King

Attr. Kraus & Haydn
B. C. Dockery

O Worship the King

Attr. Kraus & Haydn
B. C. Dockery

♩ = 102

Piano

Score

Onward, Christian Soldiers

Arthur S. Sullivan
B. C. Dockery

Flute 1

Onward, Christian Soldiers

Arthur S. Sullivan
B. C. Dockery

Flute 2

Onward, Christian Soldiers

Arthur S. Sullivan
B. C. Dockery

Onward, Christian Soldiers

Arthur S. Sullivan
B. C. Dockery

a tempo

Rock of Ages

Score

Thomas Hastings
B. C. Dockery

Rock of Ages

Rock of Ages

Flute 1

Thomas Hastings
B. C. Dockery

Rock of Ages

Flute 2

Thomas Hastings
B. C. Dockery

Rock of Ages

Piano

Thomas Hastings
B. C. Dockery

Score

Shall We Gather at the River

Robert Lowry

Arr. B. C. Dockery

Flute 1

Shall We Gather at the River

Robert Lowry
Arr. B. C. Dockery

Flute 2

Shall We Gather at the River

Robert Lowry
Arr. B. C. Dockery

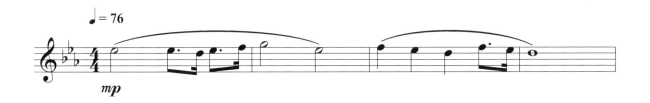

Shall We Gather at the River

Robert Lowry
Arr. B. C. Dockery

Tell Me the Story of Jesus

John R. Sweney
arr. B. C. Dockery

©2022

Tell Me the Story of Jesus

John R. Sweney
arr. B. C. Dockery

Flute 1

Tell Me the Story of Jesus

John R. Sweney
arr. B. C. Dockery

Flute 2

Tell Me the Story of Jesus

John R. Sweney
arr. B. C. Dockery

The Old Rugged Cross

George Bennard
arr. B. C. Dockery

The Old Rugged Cross

The Old Rugged Cross

Flute 1

George Bennard
arr. B. C. Dockery

The Old Rugged Cross

Flute 2

George Bennard
arr. B. C. Dockery

The Old Rugged Cross

George Bennard
arr. B. C. Dockery

Piano

There Is a Fountain

Traditional
arr. B. C. Dockery

There Is a Fountain

Flute 1

Traditional
arr. B. C. Dockery

There Is a Fountain

Flute 2

Traditional
arr. B. C. Dockery

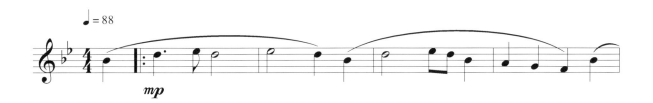

There Is a Fountain

Traditional
arr. B. C. Dockery

To God Be the Glory

Score

William H. Doane

B. C. Dockery

To God Be the Glory

To God Be the Glory

Flute 1

William H. Doane
B. C. Dockery

To God Be the Glory

Flute 2

William H. Doane
B. C. Dockery

To God Be the Glory

Piano

William H. Doane
B. C. Dockery

To God Be the Glory

Score

We Gather Together

Dutch Folk Tune
Arr. by B. C. Dockery

Flute 1

We Gather Together

Dutch Folk Tune
Arr. by B. C. Dockery

Flute 2

We Gather Together

Dutch Folk Tune
Arr. by B. C. Dockery

We Gather Together

Dutch Folk Tune
Arr. by B. C. Dockery

Were You There

Traditional
arr. B. C. Dockery

Were You There

Flute 1

Were You There

Traditional
arr. B. C. Dockery

Flute 2

Were You There

Traditional
arr. B. C. Dockery

Were You There

Traditional
arr. B. C. Dockery

What a Friend We Have in Jesus

Score

Charles C. Converse
B. C. Dockery

Arr. ©2022

What a Friend We Have in Jesus

Flute 1

Charles C. Converse
B. C. Dockery

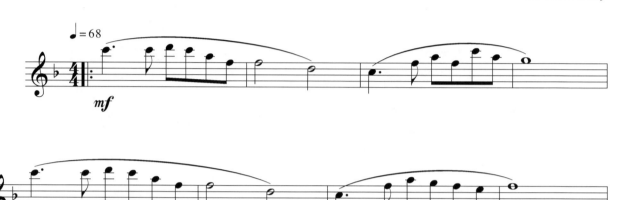

What a Friend We Have in Jesus

Flute 2

Charles C. Converse
B. C. Dockery

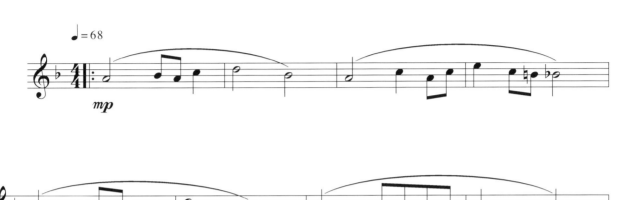

Arr. ©2022

What a Friend We Have in Jesus

Piano

Charles C. Converse
B. C. Dockery

Arr. ©2022

Score

What Wondrous Love Is This

Anonymous
Arr. by B. C. Dockery

Flute 1

What Wondrous Love Is This

Anonymous
Arr. by B. C. Dockery

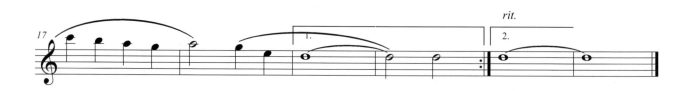

Flute 2

What Wondrous Love Is This

Anonymous
Arr. by B. C. Dockery

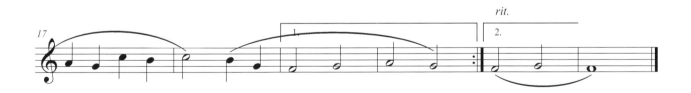

What Wondrous Love Is This

Anonymous
Arr. by B. C. Dockery

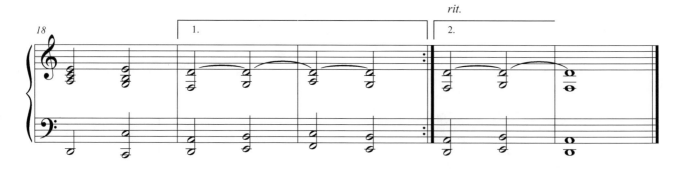

When I Survey the Wondrous Cross

Lowell Mason
arr. B. C. Dockery

When I Survey the Wondrous Cross

Flute 1

Lowell Mason
arr. B. C. Dockery

When I Survey the Wondrous Cross

Flute 2

Lowell Mason
arr. B. C. Dockery

When I Survey the Wondrous Cross

Lowell Mason
arr. B. C. Dockery